KT-369-601

SALAD DAYS

A collection of European and American salad recipes
compiled and edited by Ursel Norman
Illustrated by Derek Norman

William Morrow & Company, Inc.

New York

All rights reserved. No part of
this book may be reproduced or
utilized in any form or by any means,
electronic or mechanical, including
photocopying, recording or by any
information storage and retrieval
system, without permission in writing
from the Publisher. Inquiries should
be addressed to William Morrow and
Company, Inc., 105 Madison Ave.,
New York, N.Y. 10016

Printed in Great Britain

Library of Congress Catalog Card Number 74-21604
ISBN 0-688-02891-8

For the Evetts

SALAD DAYS

Edited & Compiled by Ursel Norman

Illustrated by Derek Norman

WALDORF SALAD

Bon Appétit

CONTENTS

Introduction	page 6
Hints on How to make your Salad a Hit	8
The Basic Green Salad	12
Tomato Salad	14
Cucumber Salad	16
Kartoffel Salat (Potato Salad)	18
Coleslaw (Dutch Cabbage)	20
Beetroot Salad	22
Bohnensalat (Green Bean Salad)	24
Green Pepper Salad Provençale	26
Raw Cabbage Salad	28
Mushroom Salad	30
Waldorf Salad (Celeriac, Nuts and Fruit)	32
Salad Niçoise (Lettuce and Tuna Fish)	34
Caesar Salad (Lettuce and Bread)	36
Hering Salat (Herring Salad)	38
Spanish Salad (Orange and Onion)	40
Chef's Salad (Lettuce and Cooked Meats)	42
Spinach Salad	44
Russian Salad (Cooked Meats and Vegetables)	46
Watercress Salad	48
Greek Salad (Lettuce, Vegetables and Cheese)	50
Flemish Endive Salad	52
Italian Summer Salad (Asparagus, Beans and Artichoke Hearts)	54
Salmon and Avocado Salad	56
Mexican Gazpacho Salad (Cucumber, Mushroom and Onion)	58
Shrimp Salad	60
Crab Salad Louis	62
Salad Dressings	64

INTRODUCTION

The Salad! A bowl of luscious, fresh greens coated with a smooth, subtle dressing. Or raw vegetables, marinated and flavored with a hint of spice or herbs. Such are the delights that can accompany the gourmet meal and family fare alike.

The salad in one form or another is a creation of infinite variety, always crisp and fresh, winter and summer alike. The sensitive palate demands a salad to accompany most meals to complement and enhance their flavor – not always a basic green salad, but one frequently making use of seasonal vegetables to give further color and imagination to a meal.

Salad Days is a collection of salad recipes and ideas that I hope will stimulate the reader into discovering the delights of the salad – a delight to the eye as well as to the palate. Also, for those people who are already salad devotees, I hope the variety will give them renewed interest, especially with the inclusion of many European salads with which they may not be familiar.

A good salad doesn't just happen. A lot of love and attention has to go into its preparation. Handle it gently at all times! You will be rewarded by maximum crispness. The actual tossing of the finally assembled ingredients is for many people quite a ritual, something usually done at the dinner table, with infinite care being taken not to bruise a single leaf.

The art of the salad is truly underrated. The pure tenderness of fresh greens stimulates and refreshes the palate so that what might accompany or follow a salad can be more fully appreciated. There is a kind of sincerity about a fresh salad that escapes definition – the most natural of foods eaten when, ideally, they are at their best and most nutritious –

like the very humble yet versatile Green Salad, a classic recipe, or Chef's Salad, an American classic. All the salads in this book are classics of one kind or another, all from different parts of the world, all with their own individual tastes and characteristics.

I have tried to give emphasis to the use and suitability of certain vegetables at certain times of the year. When fresh, seasonal vegetables are logically at their best and cheapest. This is an added bonus, but by no means a prerequisite to the preparation of a fine salad.

The format of this book is designed for ease of use and understanding, so that the reader has an immediate indication of what the finished dish looks like. And the visual step-by-step instructions convey the ease with which they can be made. The introduction to each recipe will give a clue as to the kind of taste to expect and with what it might best be served.

Finally, whatever your motivation for discovering the salad, or re-discovering it, I trust that it will add color, imagination, and enjoyment to your cooking and eating. For that is what the delights of the salad are about.

Bon appétit!

Ursel Norman

Derek Norman

Chicago

HINTS ON HOW TO MAKE YOUR SALAD A HIT

THE DO'S & DON'TS

In order that you may get the most out of your salad, the following hints will help to give guidance on the selection of ingredients and their preparation.

Lettuce
Handle it gently at all times! I have been horrified only too often to see a greengrocer stuff a tender head of lettuce into too small a paper bag, causing it to bruise. Bruises are waste – especially with Boston and romaine lettuce. These are especially fragile, Iceberg and chicory are less so.

Always wash the lettuce well, but make sure it is completely dry before tossing it with vinaigrette dressing because the dressing will not adhere to wet leaves. The best way to do this is to wrap the washed leaves in a towel (or paper towel) and leave them in the refrigerator for 2–3 hours. The towel helps to soak up the water, and the salad will

Iceberg

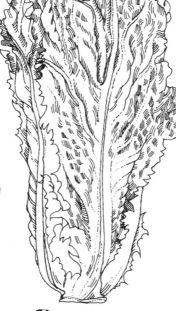

Romaine

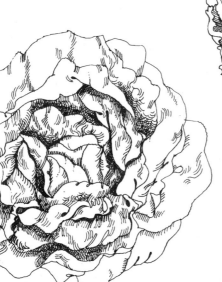

Boston Lettuce

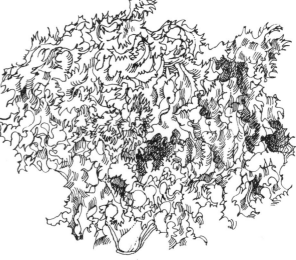

Chicory

The four most popular lettuces in America

8

come out crisp and dry. The dark in the refrigerator is also an advantage because light tends to make lettuce leaves wilt.

Another way to dry lettuce is to shake the washed leaves in a wire basket or a colander. But be gentle – don't bruise them.

Never cut lettuce with a knife, always tear it into bite-size pieces. This gives the leaves a greater absorbency along the tear.

It is best not to toss the salad until just before serving – preferably at the dinner table – since it will go limp quite quickly once it comes into contact with the oil (I cheat sometimes, when I have a lot of last-minute cooking to do. I make up the dressing in a bowl, pile the dried lettuce leaves loosely on top, and leave it in the refrigerator, covered with a paper towel, for an hour or even longer. Then all it needs is tossing, immediately before serving.)

Cucumber

Cucumbers are often bitter at the blossom end. Therefore make it a habit to cut the cucumber in half first, and peel it from the cut end to within $\frac{1}{2}$ inch of the ends. Thus you avoid pulling the bitterness all through the cucumber. Also, cucumbers shed a lot of water when they come into contact with salt, therefore it is advisable to sprinkle the peeled, sliced cucumber with some salt, leaving it to drain for at least $\frac{1}{2}$ hour in a colander. Then rinse off the salt, making sure the slices are quite dry before mixing them with the dressing.

Garlic

Some people find the use of garlic objectionable, therefore it is listed in most recipes as being optional. Only when it is not listed as optional would I suggest you really must use it, for this is the only way to catch the authentic flavor of some of these classic salads. Could it be that the smell of garlic follows you around? On your chopping board, your chopping knife, your fingers? Try sprinkling some salt on your chopping board, then dip your knife into it. Then cut or crush your garlic clove in the salt. You won't smell a thing! Sometimes it is enough to just rub a salad bowl with a cut clove of garlic; this way you don't actually eat it. Another way to give a salad a slight garlic flavor is the French way of rubbing a piece of stale bread with a cut clove of garlic and then tossing it around with the greens and the dressing. (Remove the bread before serving the salad.) This piece of bread is known as a *chapon*.

Oil

Most cookbooks will have you believe that only olive oil will do. Authentic vinaigrette dressing does indeed call for olive oil, but actually any oil found on your supermarket shelf can be used. You might even prefer it to the very heavy olive oil. Only in recipes where I specifically recommend the use of olive oil would I strongly suggest you use it for maximum authenticity.

Vinegar

The same applies to vinegar. Red or white wine vinegars are undoubtedly the most delicious. Try buying the unflavored ones though. That way you can add your own flavorings, either herbs from your garden or dried ones off your kitchen shelf. This lets you bring more variety into your dressings. Ordinary vinegars are also quite delicious, and certainly much cheaper, and added herbs give them flavor. You will find that I have used mostly ordinary vinegars in my recipes.

Instead of vinegar you can also use an equal quantity of fresh lemon juice. This can make a very pleasant change. If the lemon dressing seems a little sour, add a sprinkle of sugar to it.

Salad Bowls

The ideal salad bowl for tossed salads is a large wooden one, with a large wooden spoon and fork. The softness of the wooden utensils is least likely to bruise the salad. These bowls should be washed quickly in warm soapy water and dried straight away. Never leave one to soak.

Glass bowls are also very attractive, as are china or ceramic ones. Just make sure they are not made of a porous material; in other words, they must be well glazed. Naturally you would not let vinegar touch silver or metal bowls.

Salad Dressings

For tossed green or mixed salads only a vinaigrette dressing (oil, vinegar or lemon) is acceptable. I tend to have a personal dislike for all the creamy concoctions in bottles and jars. I find home-made ones acceptable, though only on Iceberg lettuce, since this is the only kind of lettuce that won't collapse under a heavy dressing. A salad is designed to stimulate the palate, therefore a salad with a creamy dressing tends to have the reverse effect. However, for those who can't live without creamy dressings, I have given recipes of some of the more popular ones on page 64.

As regards mayonnaise, I would like to stress that only a *good* commercial one should be used. Or better still, make your own. The recipe is on page 64.

Never, *never* use any kind of commercial salad dressing for any of the recipes in this book.

When and How to Serve

Salads can start a meal and be served as an hors d'oeuvre, go with a meal and accompany the main dish, or come after the main course. When eaten before a meal as an hors d'oeuvre, the salad should be served on individual chilled plates and eaten with just a fork. The same applies to salads eaten after the main course. Salads eaten with the main course may also be served on small individual plates or bowls and placed at the top left-hand side of the dinner plate. It is also quite acceptable to serve a salad on the same plate as the main course, especially with rice or pasta dishes, when no other vegetable is served.

One note of advice: always serve a salad at some point during a dinner party. Your guests will appreciate the fresh, cool change during the meal.

And, diet-conscious or not, a salad can make an ideal meal in itself.

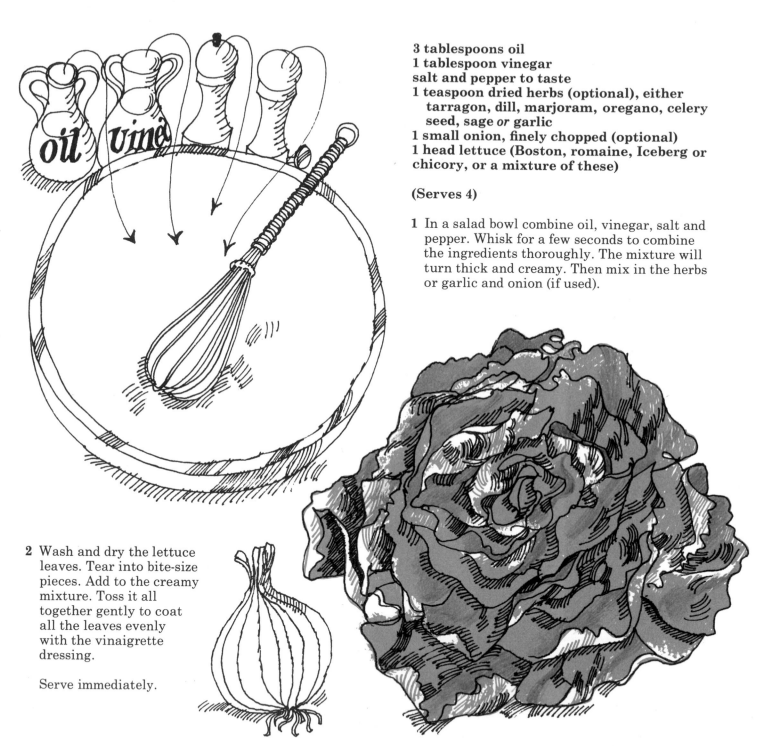

3 tablespoons oil
1 tablespoon vinegar
salt and pepper to taste
1 teaspoon dried herbs (optional), either
   tarragon, dill, marjoram, oregano, celery
   seed, sage *or* garlic
1 small onion, finely chopped (optional)
1 head lettuce (Boston, romaine, Iceberg or
chicory, or a mixture of these)

(Serves 4)

1 In a salad bowl combine oil, vinegar, salt and
   pepper. Whisk for a few seconds to combine
   the ingredients thoroughly. The mixture will
   turn thick and creamy. Then mix in the herbs
   or garlic and onion (if used).

2 Wash and dry the lettuce
   leaves. Tear into bite-size
   pieces. Add to the creamy
   mixture. Toss it all
   together gently to coat
   all the leaves evenly
   with the vinaigrette
   dressing.

   Serve immediately.

Note:
The Green Salad is also the basis for making a
Mixed Salad – simply add your own choice of
vegetables (tomato, cucumber, radishes,
watercress, mustard greens, red and green peppers,
sliced mushrooms, etc.)

The Basic Green Salad

This is probably the world's most popular and versatile salad.
The classic French vinaigrette dressing gives it a tangy kind of
flavor, guaranteed to refresh the palate. As a side dish the green
salad will accompany any main course. It is a must with all rice and
pasta dishes.

When you are not sure of a vegetable to go with a certain dish,
the green salad will always prove an excellent choice.

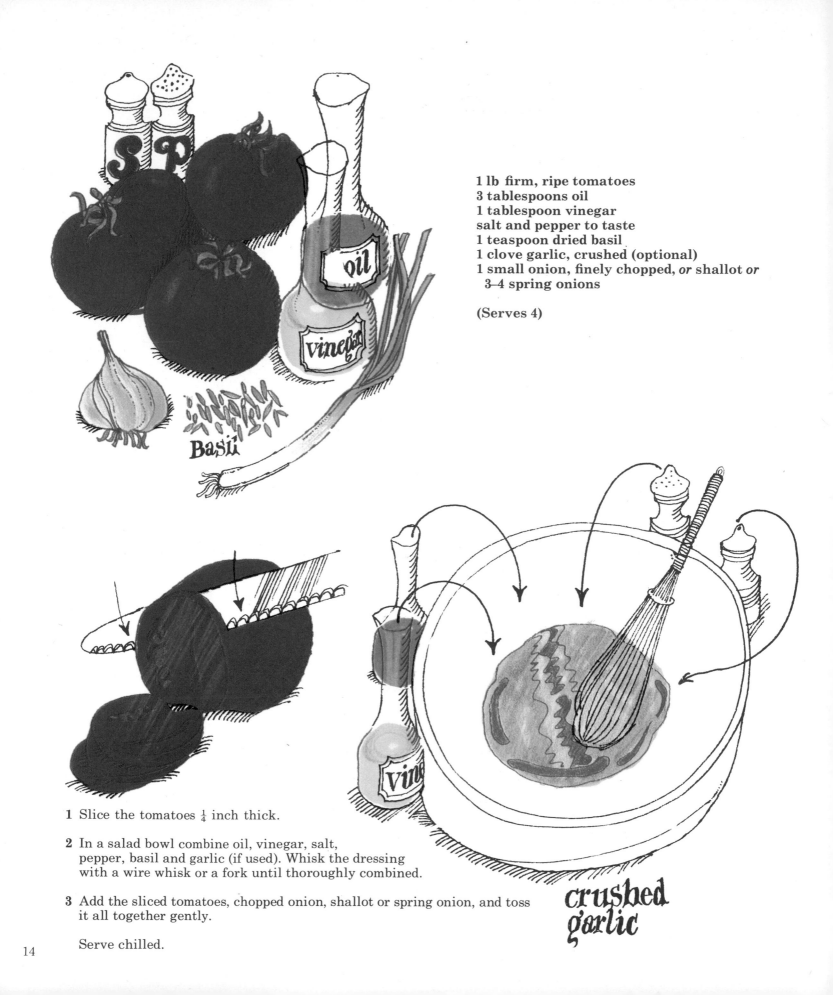

1 lb firm, ripe tomatoes
3 tablespoons oil
1 tablespoon vinegar
salt and pepper to taste
1 teaspoon dried basil
1 clove garlic, crushed (optional)
1 small onion, finely chopped, *or* shallot *or*
  3–4 spring onions

(Serves 4)

Basil

1 Slice the tomatoes $\frac{1}{4}$ inch thick.

2 In a salad bowl combine oil, vinegar, salt,
   pepper, basil and garlic (if used). Whisk the dressing
   with a wire whisk or a fork until thoroughly combined.

3 Add the sliced tomatoes, chopped onion, shallot or spring onion, and toss
   it all together gently.

   Serve chilled.

crushed
garlic

TOMATO SALAD

Especially fine in summer when tomatoes are at their peak. Cool and juicy, it is ideal for serving with fried dishes – particularly steak, chops or fish. A bowl of tomato salad will add a brilliant splash of color to the dinner table.

A touch of basil, together with the garlic, highlights the authentic Continental flavor of this recipe.

1 cucumber
2 tablespoons oil
2 tablespoons vinegar
salt and pepper to taste
$\frac{1}{4}$ teaspoon dried dill
3–4 spring onions, chopped, *or* 1 small onion, chopped
1 tablespoon heavy cream *or* evaporated milk

(Serves 4)

1 Peel the cucumber (see page 9) and slice into very, very thin slices. Place them in a colander. Sprinkle a little salt over the slices and leave them to drain for 30 minutes. Rinse them with cold water and dry thoroughly with paper towels.

2 In a bowl whisk together the oil, vinegar, salt, pepper and dill. Mix in the spring onions and the cream.

3 Toss the cucumber slices in the bowl to coat them evenly with the dressing.

Serve chilled.

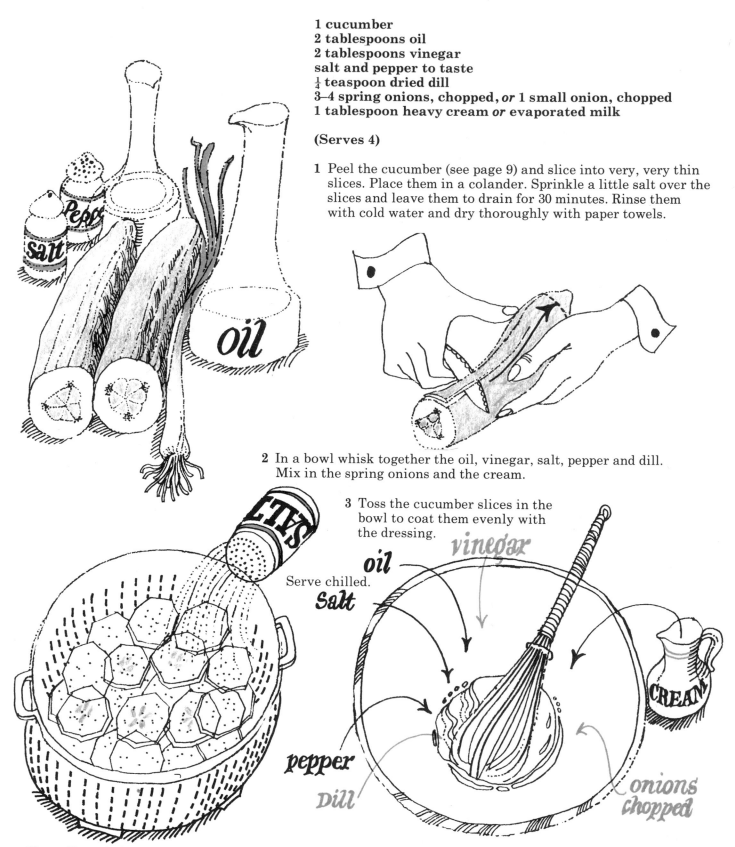

Note: By omitting the draining procedure (preparing the dressing first and then slicing the peeled cucumber into it), the dressing will be diluted by the juice from the cucumber. This also makes a delicious salad, and children love the juice.

CUCUMBER SALAD

This beautifully juicy salad with a taste of spring is very smooth on the palate and is ideal with rice dishes or with buttered, new potatoes. The addition of dill gives it a slightly sweet and very delicate taste. A favorite with children.

1 lb good, small red potatoes
2 tablespoons vinegar
½ teaspoon sugar
salt and pepper to taste

(Serves 3 or 4)

1 small onion, finely chopped
1 heaped tablespoon chopped gherkin
    (optional)
3–4 heaped tablespoons good mayonnaise
1 hardboiled egg, cut into wedges
a little chopped parsley

1 Leave the skin on the potatoes. Boil them until tender in salted water. Drain and leave them to cool.

2 Put the vinegar, sugar, salt and pepper into a bowl and whisk to combine. Add chopped onion and gherkin (if used) and the peeled, thinly sliced potatoes. (Halve the larger potatoes to keep all the slices small.)

3 Add the mayonnaise, mix it all well, and garnish with the hardboiled egg and chopped parsley.

4 Leave to marinate for 1 hour.

Note: This salad will keep for a day or two if kept tightly covered in a refrigerator. To freshen it up again, toss in 1 tablespoon of boiling water before serving.

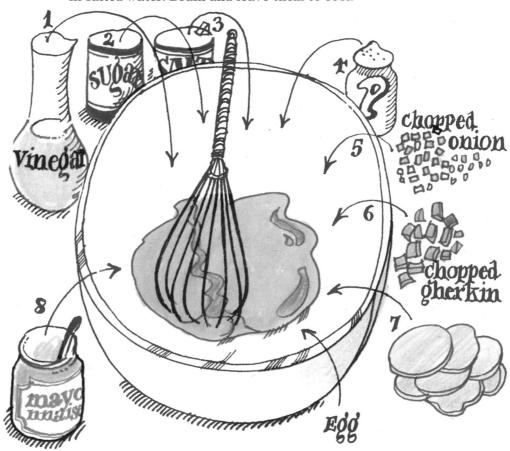

Kartoffel Salat

I always think of this salad as being distinctly German, and
this is an authentic German recipe. The taste is especially
fine with frankfurters, any cold meat, and, would you believe it,
fried fish. (You may find it even more to your liking than french fries.)
In Germany no picnic is complete without the potato salad.

1 small white cabbage, about 1 lb
salt and pepper to taste
½ teaspoon sugar
2 tablespoons vinegar
1 small green pepper, seeded and sliced (optional)
1 teaspoon celery seed (optional)
3 tablespoons good mayonnaise
chopped chives *or* parsley

(Serves 4–6)

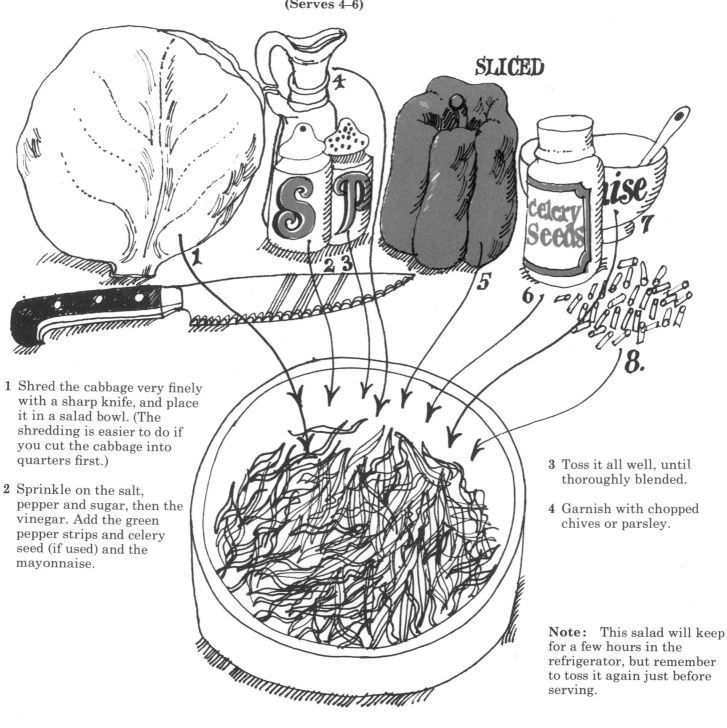

SLICED

1 Shred the cabbage very finely with a sharp knife, and place it in a salad bowl. (The shredding is easier to do if you cut the cabbage into quarters first.)

2 Sprinkle on the salt, pepper and sugar, then the vinegar. Add the green pepper strips and celery seed (if used) and the mayonnaise.

3 Toss it all well, until thoroughly blended.

4 Garnish with chopped chives or parsley.

Note: This salad will keep for a few hours in the refrigerator, but remember to toss it again just before serving.

COLESLAW

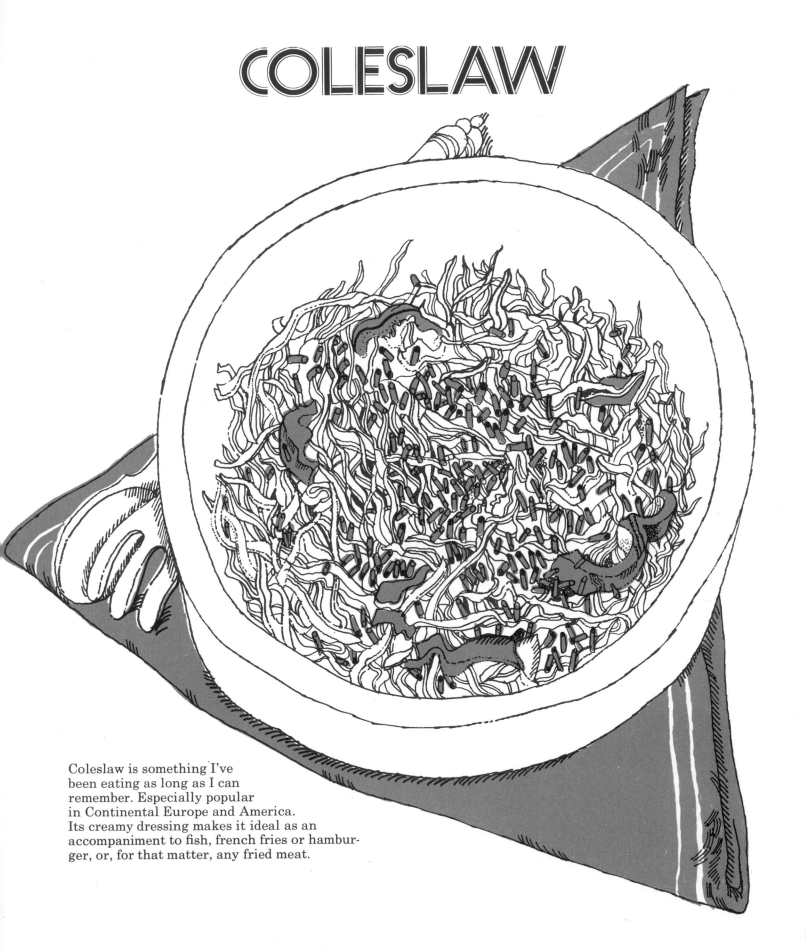

Coleslaw is something I've
been eating as long as I can
remember. Especially popular
in Continental Europe and America.
Its creamy dressing makes it ideal as an
accompaniment to fish, french fries or hambur-
ger, or, for that matter, any fried meat.

2 lb beetroot
1 large onion, cut into rings
$\frac{1}{2}$ cup vinegar
$\frac{1}{2}$ cup water
2 teaspoons sugar
1 bayleaf
4 peppercorns
2 whole cloves
$\frac{1}{2}$ teaspoon salt
$\frac{1}{2}$ teaspoon caraway seeds (optional)

(Serves 4)

1 Cook the beetroot in salted water until tender, peel them, and cut them into slices.

2 Place them in a deep china or glass dish together with the onion rings.

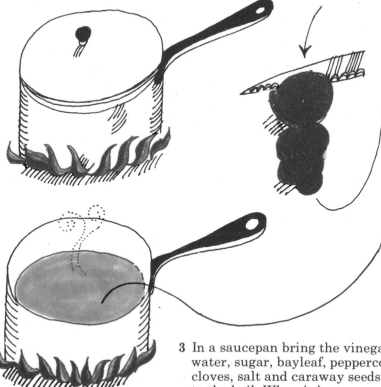

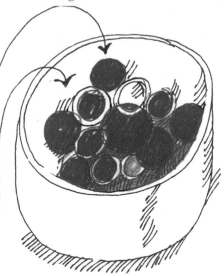

4 Leave to cool and then refrigerate until ready to use.

3 In a saucepan bring the vinegar, water, sugar, bayleaf, peppercorns, cloves, salt and caraway seeds to the boil. When it just reaches the boiling point, pour this marinade over the beetroot and onions.

Note: This salad will keep for about a week if tightly covered and kept in the refrigerator.

Beetroot Salad

This recipe was one of my grandmother's favorites. The marinade gives this salad its unique taste and distinctive, old-fashioned kind of flavor. Especially good with cold meats, fried fish and potato dishes. (In England the greengrocer always sells beetroot already boiled, which makes making this salad much easier; alas this is not the case in the States.)

For weight watchers – almost zero calories.

1 lb green string beans *or* 1 large can cut green beans
3 tablespoons oil
1 tablespoon vinegar
salt and pepper to taste
1 small onion, finely chopped, *or* shallot *or* 3–4 spring onions
½ teaspoon dried tarragon, oregano, dill *or* garlic (optional)
1 sprig of parsley for garnish

(Serves 4)

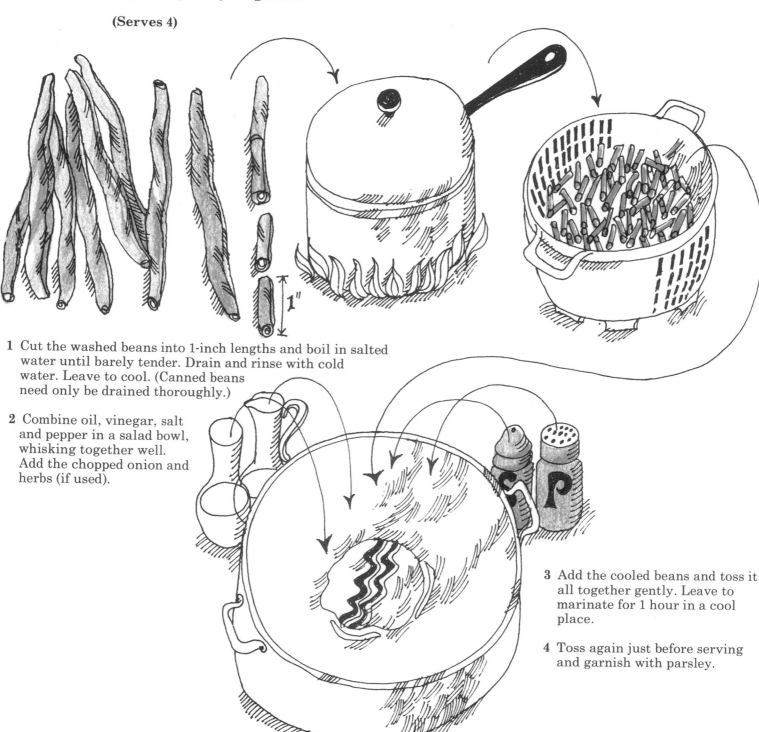

1 Cut the washed beans into 1-inch lengths and boil in salted
   water until barely tender. Drain and rinse with cold
   water. Leave to cool. (Canned beans
   need only be drained thoroughly.)

2 Combine oil, vinegar, salt
   and pepper in a salad bowl,
   whisking together well.
   Add the chopped onion and
   herbs (if used).

3 Add the cooled beans and toss it
   all together gently. Leave to
   marinate for 1 hour in a cool
   place.

4 Toss again just before serving
   and garnish with parsley.

Bohnensalat

An old German salad. This is my own recipe,
inherited from my mother, who inherited it
from her mother, who I suspect inherited it
from her mother. However, this particular recipe
I like to feel is distinguished by its simplicity.
Smooth and soft, it can be served instead of a vegetable
with just about any dish.

4 firm green peppers
1 clove garlic
¼ teaspoon salt
5 tablespoons olive oil
1 small tin pimientos
  or add 1 red pepper to the green ones
a few pitted black olives

(Serves 4)

1 To peel the peppers spear them on a
   fork and scorch the skin over a flame
   until it turns quite black, then
   scrape it off with a knife.

2 Cut the peeled peppers into
   quarters and remove all the seeds.
   Cut them into strips.

3 Crush the clove of garlic into the
   salt until it turns almost to a
   liquid, then with a wire whisk beat
   in the oil in a thin, steady stream.

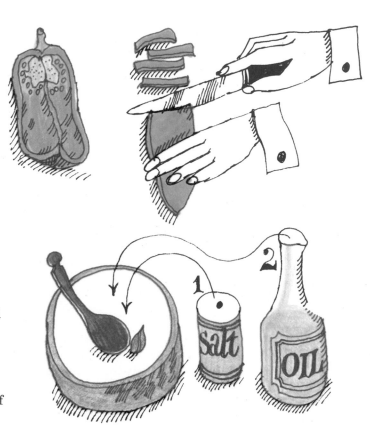

4 Arrange the peppers attractively on a
   platter, scatter the pimientos (or the red
   pepper strips) over them, and pour the
   dressing over. Garnish with the olives.
   Cover the dish and leave the flavors to
   mingle for 30–60 minutes.

Note: This salad will keep for 2–3 days if
kept tightly covered in a refrigerator.

Green Pepper Salad Provençale

A truly magnificent French recipe, a Mediterranean delight. The grace and flavor of this salad complements almost any meal. Or alternatively it can be served as part of an hors d'oeuvre. You will find its taste smooth, soft, and unusually different.

½ lb firm green or white cabbage, thinly shredded
½ lb red cabbage, thinly shredded
salt and pepper to taste
1 green pepper, seeded and cut into strips (optional)
1 small onion, thinly sliced
4 tablespoons oil
2 tablespoons vinegar
1 tablespoon chopped parsley

(Serves 4–6)

1 Cut both cabbages into quarters and shred them very thinly with a sharp knife. Discard the core.

2 Place the shredded cabbage in a bowl, add the salt, pepper, green pepper strips and onion rings. Toss lightly.

3 In a screwtop jar combine oil and vinegar and shake until thoroughly blended.

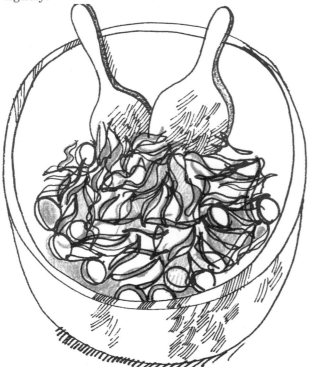

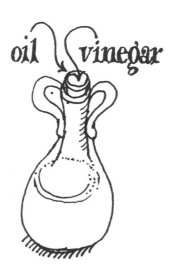

4 Pour the dressing over the salad, toss it thoroughly, and refrigerate until ready to use.

5 Just before serving toss it again lightly and sprinkle with the chopped parsley.

RAW CABBAGE SALAD

An extremely crunchy, tangy and crisp salad, highly nutritious, that can be eaten any time of the year. The cabbage salad has a certain earthiness which is always refreshing and stimulating to the palate. It makes a fine winter salad.

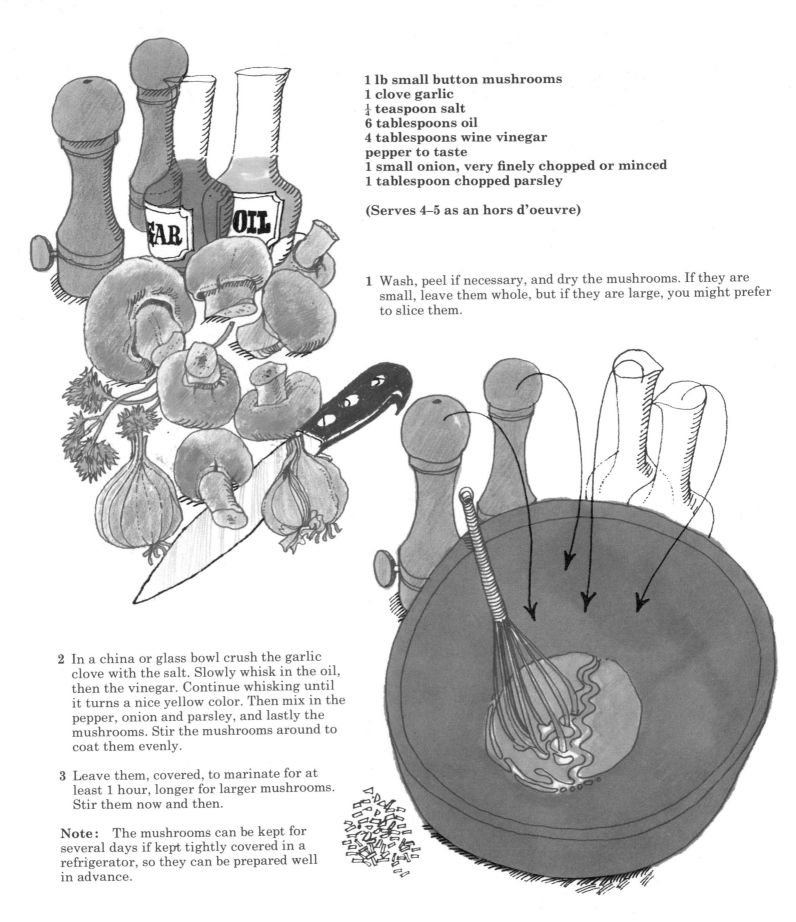

1 lb small button mushrooms
1 clove garlic
$\frac{1}{4}$ teaspoon salt
6 tablespoons oil
4 tablespoons wine vinegar
pepper to taste
1 small onion, very finely chopped or minced
1 tablespoon chopped parsley

(Serves 4–5 as an hors d'oeuvre)

1 Wash, peel if necessary, and dry the mushrooms. If they are small, leave them whole, but if they are large, you might prefer to slice them.

2 In a china or glass bowl crush the garlic clove with the salt. Slowly whisk in the oil, then the vinegar. Continue whisking until it turns a nice yellow color. Then mix in the pepper, onion and parsley, and lastly the mushrooms. Stir the mushrooms around to coat them evenly.

3 Leave them, covered, to marinate for at least 1 hour, longer for larger mushrooms. Stir them now and then.

Note: The mushrooms can be kept for several days if kept tightly covered in a refrigerator, so they can be prepared well in advance.

Mushroom Salad

A magnificent and unusual taste. The marinade "cooks" the mushrooms to leave them soft and absolutely delicious. Mushroom salad can be served as an hors d'oeuvre, or as part of a buffet.

1 small celeriac
1½ oz chopped walnuts
½ lb green grapes, seeds removed
1 small eating apple
juice of 1 lemon
4 tablespoons good mayonnaise
salt and pepper to taste
chives or parsley, chopped, for garnish

(Serves 4)

1 Boil the celeriac in salted water until tender;
at least 30 minutes. Test as for potatoes.

2 Peel off the skin and cut into
½-inch cubes.

chopped
walnuts.

Lemon
Juice

Deseeded grapes.

3 Place the cubes in a salad bowl. Add the roughly
chopped walnuts and the seeded grapes. Peel the
apple and cut it into small pieces. Coat the apple
pieces with lemon juice to prevent their discoloring. Add to the salad bowl.

4
Make up a dressing of the mayonnaise, leftover lemon juice,
salt and pepper. Add the dressing to the salad, and toss it all
together lightly but thoroughly.

5 Refrigerate until ready to use, then
sprinkle on the chives or parsley.

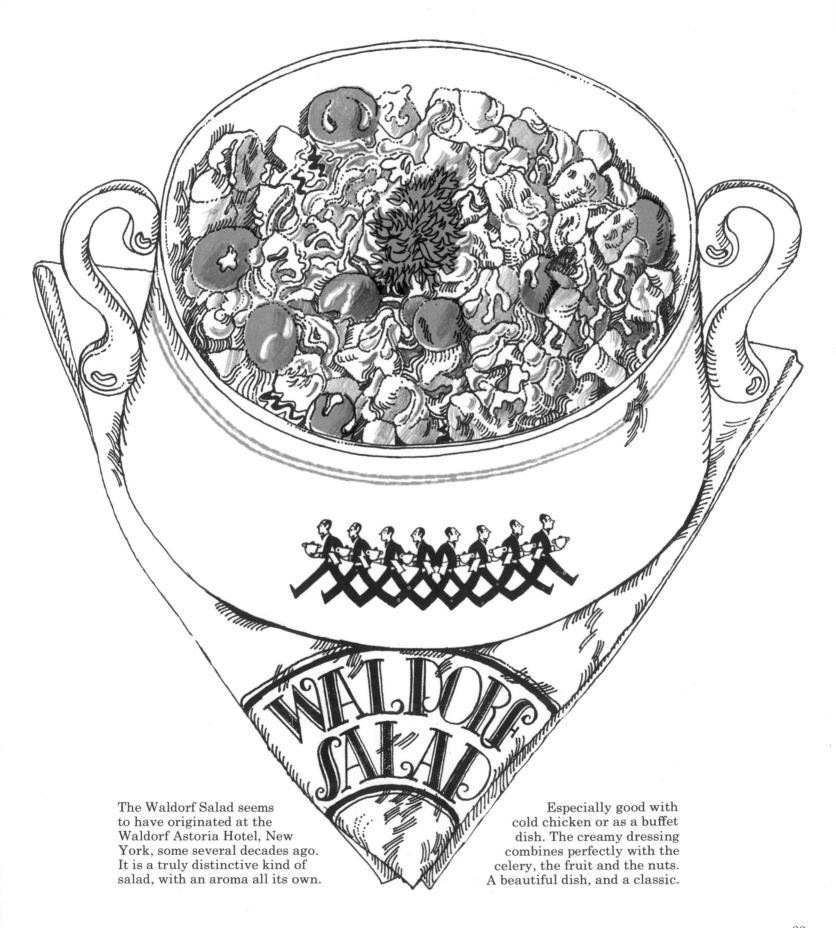

WALDORF SALAD

The Waldorf Salad seems to have originated at the Waldorf Astoria Hotel, New York, some several decades ago. It is a truly distinctive kind of salad, with an aroma all its own.

Especially good with cold chicken or as a buffet dish. The creamy dressing combines perfectly with the celery, the fruit and the nuts. A beautiful dish, and a classic.

2 lettuce hearts
2 cans tuna fish
10 or so pitted black olives
1 onion, cut into rings
2 tomatoes, cut into wedges
¼ lb or more cooked string beans
1 green pepper, cut into strips
1 hardboiled egg, cut into wedges
½ cup olive oil
4 tablespoons white wine vinegar
¼ teaspoon dried tarragon
¼ teaspoon dried dill
salt and pepper to taste
1 clove garlic, crushed

(Serves 4 for lunch or 6 as an hors d'oeuvre)

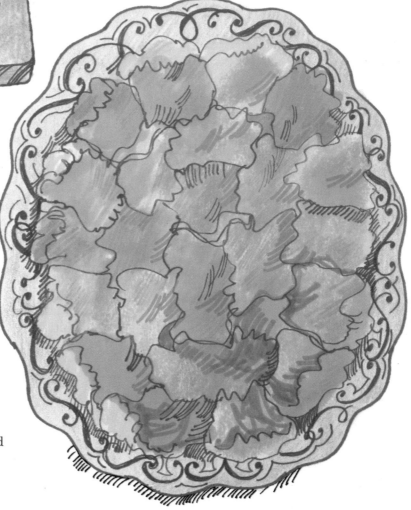

1 Wash and dry the lettuce and tear it into bite-size pieces. Line a nice platter with them.

2 Mound the tuna fish in the centre and garnish the platter attractively with olives, onion rings, tomatoes, string beans, pepper strips and wedges of hard-boiled egg.

3 Make a vinaigrette dressing from the rest of the ingredients in a screw top jar or bottle, and shake it to combine it all thoroughly.

4 Pour the dressing over the salad and serve immediately.

Note: Niçoise salad lends itself to great variations. Sometimes it can also include boiled and cubed potato, anchovy fillets, cooked artichoke bottoms or peas.

SALAD NIÇOISE

A French provincial classic, generally accepted as originating in Nice. A truly great salad that's almost a complete meal in itself.

Its combination of ingredients gives it a wholesome country character, ideal for a summer lunch. It can also be served as an hors d'oeuvre.

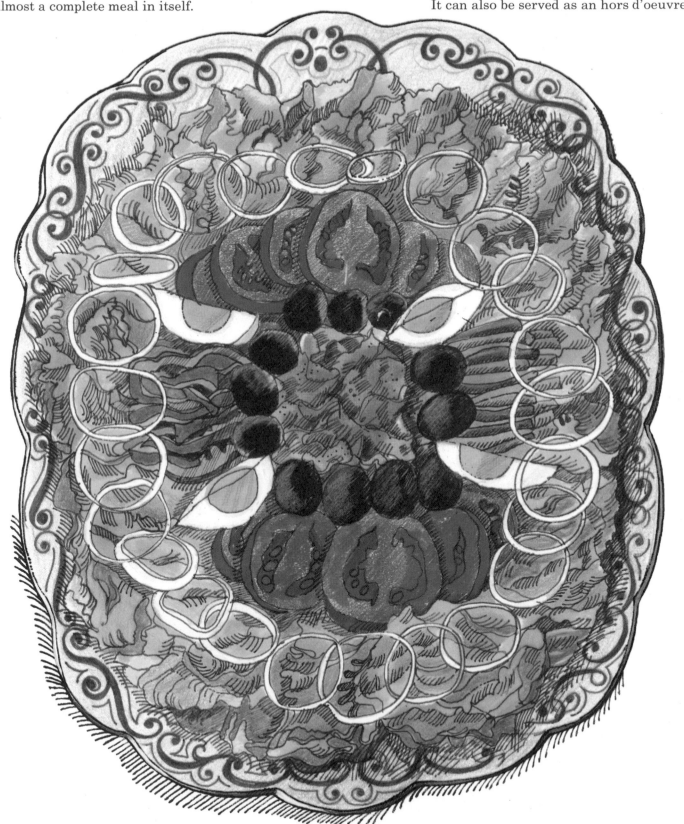

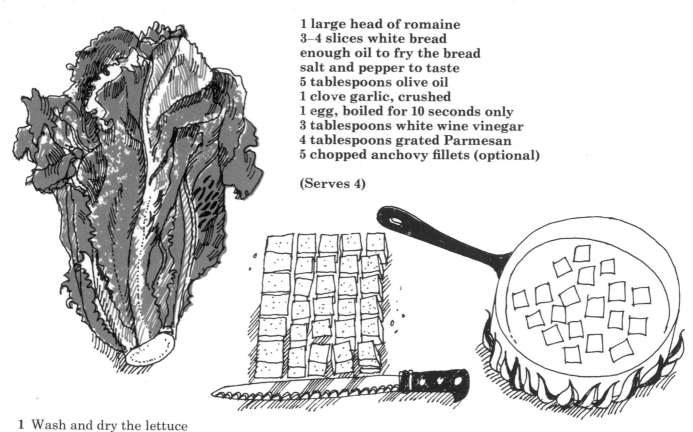

1 large head of romaine
3–4 slices white bread
enough oil to fry the bread
salt and pepper to taste
5 tablespoons olive oil
1 clove garlic, crushed
1 egg, boiled for 10 seconds only
3 tablespoons white wine vinegar
4 tablespoons grated Parmesan
5 chopped anchovy fillets (optional)

(Serves 4)

1 Wash and dry the lettuce well, wrap in a towel and refrigerate until ready to use.

2 To make *croutons*, cut the crust off and cube each slice of bread. Fry the cubes in oil until nicely browned all round.

3 Now tear the lettuce into bite-size pieces and put into a large salad bowl. Add the salt and pepper, the crushed garlic and olive oil, and toss gently.

4 Break the egg over the salad, add the vinegar and toss again lightly.

5 Sprinkle the Parmesan and anchovy fillets (if used) over it all, and toss again lightly.

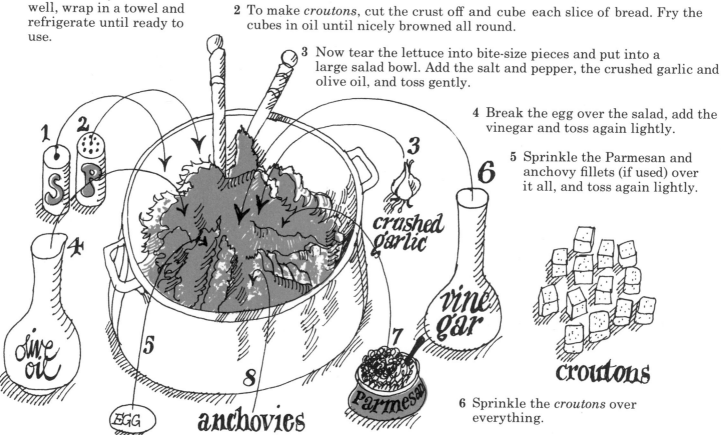

6 Sprinkle the *croutons* over everything.

Serve immediately.

Caesar Salad

A Southern California classic. The rich tender greens make a particularly crisp salad. The fresh flavor of the dressing makes it a highly distinctive dish for the connoisseur or novice alike. There are numerous variations of the Caesar Salad, but to my own knowledge this recipe is the most authentic.

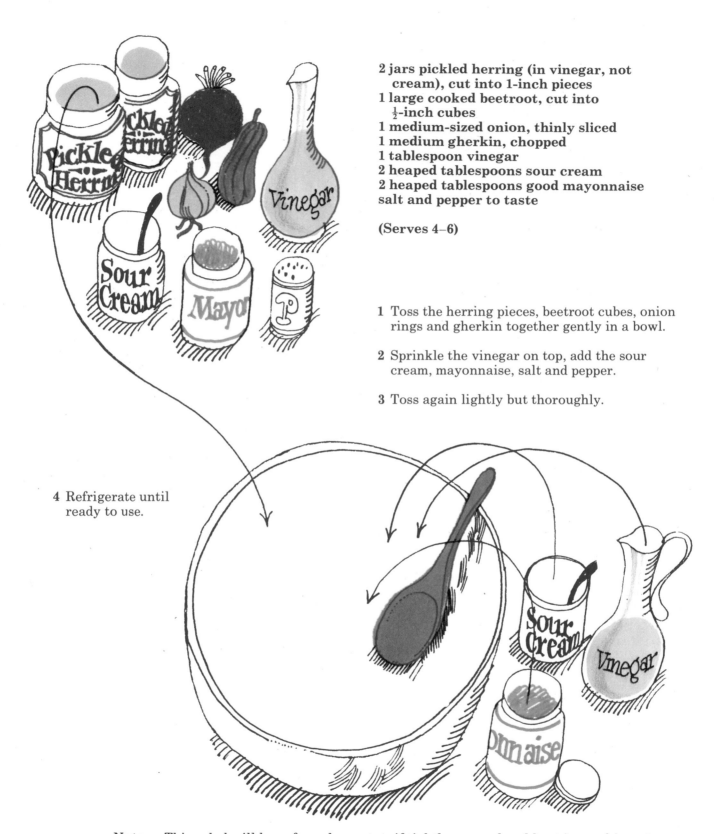

**2 jars pickled herring (in vinegar, not
  cream), cut into 1-inch pieces
1 large cooked beetroot, cut into
  ½-inch cubes
1 medium-sized onion, thinly sliced
1 medium gherkin, chopped
1 tablespoon vinegar
2 heaped tablespoons sour cream
2 heaped tablespoons good mayonnaise
salt and pepper to taste**

(Serves 4–6)

1 Toss the herring pieces, beetroot cubes, onion
rings and gherkin together gently in a bowl.

2 Sprinkle the vinegar on top, add the sour
cream, mayonnaise, salt and pepper.

3 Toss again lightly but thoroughly.

4 Refrigerate until
ready to use.

Note: This salad will keep for a day or two if tightly covered and kept in a refrigerator.

Hering Salat

A simple version of an authentic German recipe.
Creamy, fishy, and beautifully smooth. It makes an ideal hors d'oeuvre
or buffet dish. Or, as a midnight snack after a late night
out, it will help to clear your head the morning after.

1 onion, thinly sliced
1 orange, cut into segments
4 tablespoons oil
4 tablespoons vinegar
salt and pepper to taste
1 head lettuce (any kind)

(Serves 4)

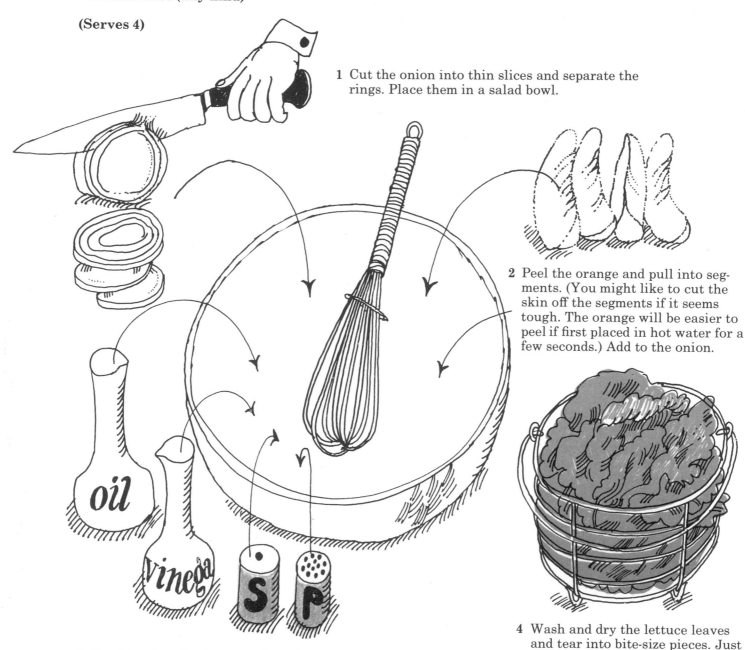

1 Cut the onion into thin slices and separate the rings. Place them in a salad bowl.

2 Peel the orange and pull into segments. (You might like to cut the skin off the segments if it seems tough. The orange will be easier to peel if first placed in hot water for a few seconds.) Add to the onion.

3 Combine the oil, vinegar, salt and pepper, and whisk until well blended. Pour this mixture over the onions and orange. Cover the bowl and leave to marinate in the refrigerator for 1 hour.

4 Wash and dry the lettuce leaves and tear into bite-size pieces. Just before serving, gently toss the lettuce in the marinade.

Serve immediately.

Spanish Salad

The orange and onion give this salad a really delightful flavour. Crisp, juicy and truly refreshing, it is a salad that can be enjoyed at any time of the year.

The combination of flavours goes well with light meat, chicken or fish.

1 head lettuce (preferably Iceberg)
½ lb cold, cooked chicken, cubed
¼ lb thick sliced ham, cubed
¼ lb cheese, cubed (any kind)
2 hardboiled eggs, cut into wedges
2 tomatoes, cut into wedges
1 bunch watercress
5 spring onions
a **Salad Dressing from page 64** *or* **the
vinaigrette dressing for Salad Niçoise,
pages 34–5**

(Serves 4)

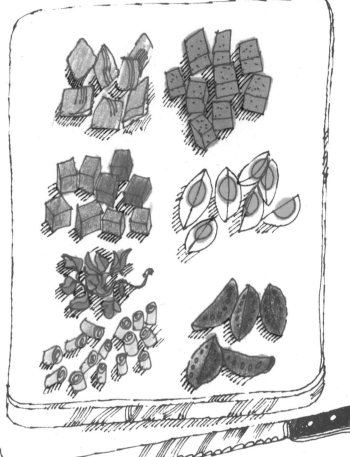

1 Wash and dry all the vegetables. Tear the
lettuce into bite-size pieces, and place in a
wide, shallow bowl or on a platter.

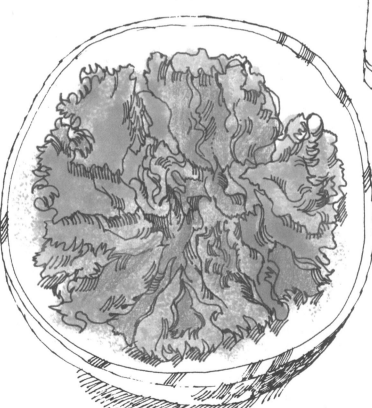

2 On top of the lettuce arrange the chicken
cubes, ham cubes, cheese cubes, egg wedges,
tomato wedges, watercress and spring onions
in an attractive pattern.

3 Pass the dressing separately in a small bowl.
Let everyone help themselves to the salad
first, and then let them pour their own
desired amount of dressing.

Chef's Salad.

Generally recognized as being American in origin, the Chef's Salad makes an ideal light lunch or supper. Try it with a glass of wine and a chunk of crusty bread. Especially fine on a hot summer's day. Its wholesome goodness also makes it a fine picnic salad.

enough raw spinach for your needs
1 small cucumber
salt
2 tablespoons red wine vinegar
4 tablespoons oil
salt and pepper to taste
a little dry mustard

(Serves 4)

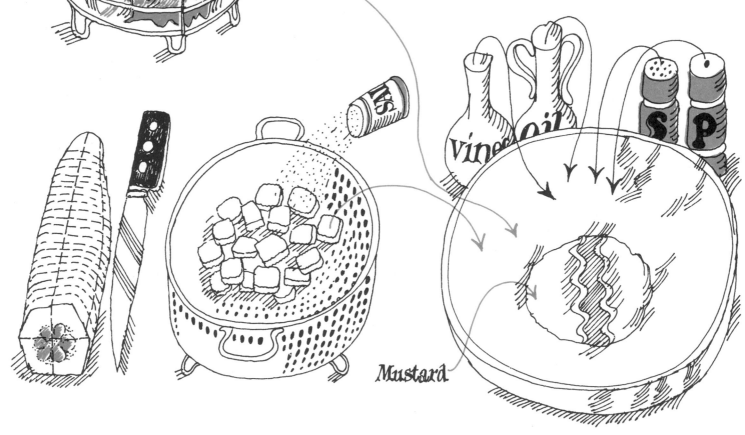

1 Wash the spinach well and clean it of any tough
   leaves and stems. Leave to dry completely.

2 Peel the cucumber and cut into small cubes and
   place them in a colander. Sprinkle on some salt
   and leave to drain for at least 30 minutes. Rinse
   with cold water and leave them to dry.

3 Mix the vinegar, oil, salt, pepper and dry
   mustard together in a salad bowl, add the
   spinach and the cucumber, and toss together
   gently but thoroughly.

   Serve immediately.

SPINACH SALAD

A salad of good, earthy character, honest and sincere. The combination of spinach and velvety cucumber, plus the dressing, gives this salad a distinctive taste all its own. Zesty, robust and highly nutritious.

Mothers might be interested to know that this is the only way I can get my children to eat spinach. An unusual accompaniment to any main course.

$\frac{1}{2}-\frac{3}{4}$ lb lean, cooked, cold meat
(leftover veal, beef, pork or lamb, cut into
julienne strips about 1 inch long
and $\frac{1}{4}$ inch wide)
1 cup cooked green peas
1 large carrot, cooked and cubed
2 cold, boiled potatoes, cubed
2 gherkins, cubed
1 medium onion, cut into julienne strips
2 tablespoons vinegar
3–4 tablespoons juice from gherkins
salt and pepper to taste
1 level teaspoon sugar
1 small carton sour cream
chopped parsley or chives for garnish

(Serves 4–6)

2 Make a marinade of vinegar, gherkin juice, salt and
pepper and the sugar, and pour it over the salad in the
bowl.

1 Place all the meat and vegetables in a
salad bowl.

3 Leave to marinate in the refrigerator for an hour or
longer, tossing it once in a while.

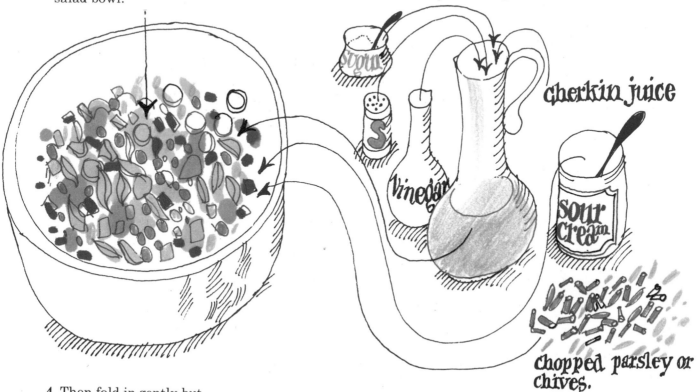

4 Then fold in gently but
thoroughly the sour cream.

5 Dust with chopped parsley or
chives.

Note: This salad will keep for a day or two if tightly covered
and kept in a refrigerator.
You can also use cooked green beans, broad beans, capers,
black or green olives, cooked beetroot or cooked mushrooms.

RUSSIAN SALAD

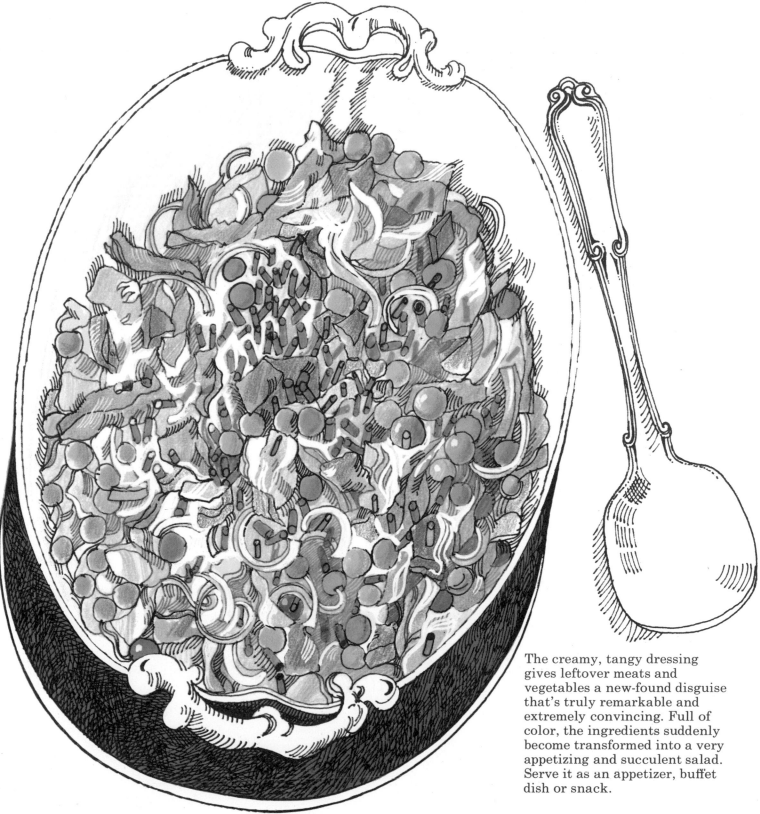

The creamy, tangy dressing gives leftover meats and vegetables a new-found disguise that's truly remarkable and extremely convincing. Full of color, the ingredients suddenly become transformed into a very appetizing and succulent salad. Serve it as an appetizer, buffet dish or snack.

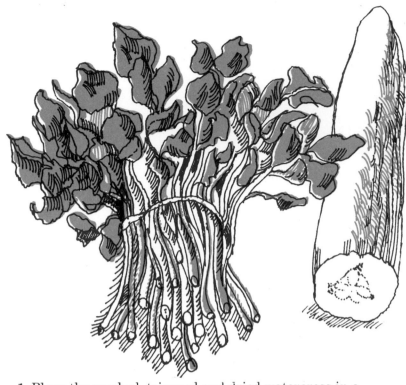

2 bunches watercress
½ cucumber, peeled and thinly sliced
4 oz blue cheese, crumbled (optional)
3 tablespoons fresh lemon juice
8 tablespoons oil
salt and pepper to taste

(Serves 4)

1 Place the washed, trimmed and dried watercress in a salad bowl, add the sliced cucumber and the crumbled cheese (if used).

2 Toss it all together.

3 Into a screwtop jar put the lemon juice, oil, salt and pepper, and shake it well until thoroughly mixed and thick and creamy.

crumbled cheese

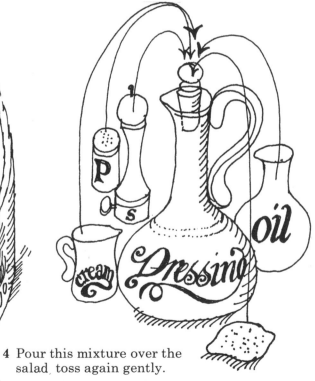

4 Pour this mixture over the salad, toss again gently.

Serve immediately

Watercress Salad

You could call this a real English salad, insofar as watercress must be more readily available in England than anywhere else. The tangy lemon dressing gives this salad a delicate taste. Ideal as an accompaniment to any main course.

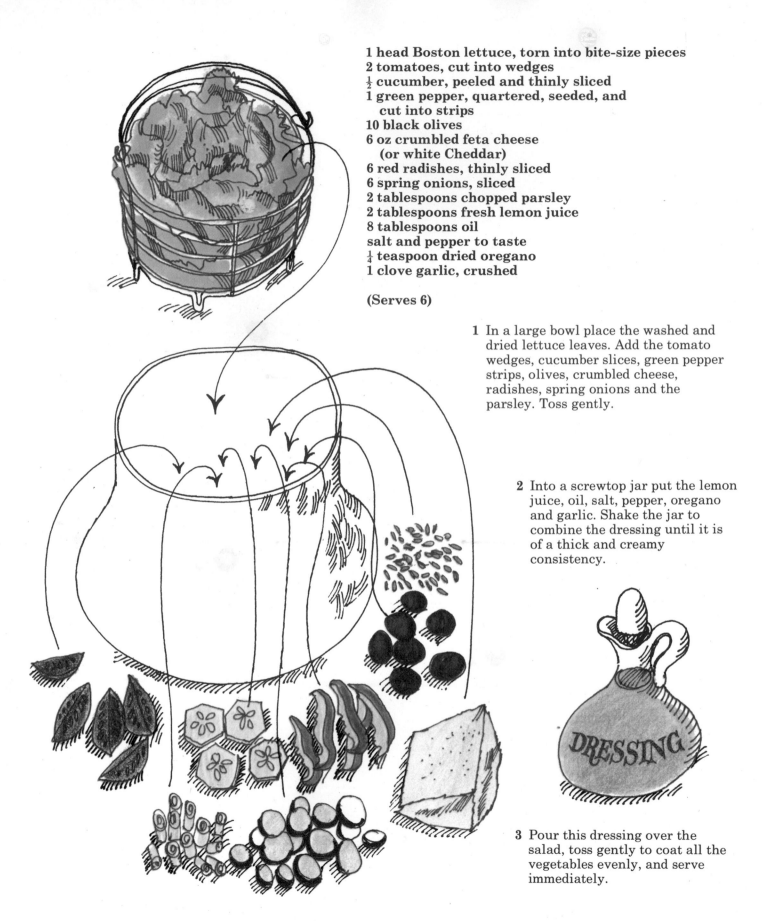

1 head Boston lettuce, torn into bite-size pieces
2 tomatoes, cut into wedges
½ cucumber, peeled and thinly sliced
1 green pepper, quartered, seeded, and
   cut into strips
10 black olives
6 oz crumbled feta cheese
   (or white Cheddar)
6 red radishes, thinly sliced
6 spring onions, sliced
2 tablespoons chopped parsley
2 tablespoons fresh lemon juice
8 tablespoons oil
salt and pepper to taste
¼ teaspoon dried oregano
1 clove garlic, crushed

(Serves 6)

1 In a large bowl place the washed and dried lettuce leaves. Add the tomato wedges, cucumber slices, green pepper strips, olives, crumbled cheese, radishes, spring onions and the parsley. Toss gently.

2 Into a screwtop jar put the lemon juice, oil, salt, pepper, oregano and garlic. Shake the jar to combine the dressing until it is of a thick and creamy consistency.

DRESSING

3 Pour this dressing over the salad, toss gently to coat all the vegetables evenly, and serve immediately.

GREEK SALAD

As refreshing and stimulating as it looks. A perfect blend of vegetables and cheese. The lemon dressing gives it a good tangy taste. The feta cheese gives an authentic Mediterranean flavor. However, if feta cheese is not available, do not despair, white Cheddar makes an adequate substitute.

Excellent as a first course or as a side dish. A favorite in our household.

½ lb thick sliced bacon
oil for frying bacon
6 heads endive
2 hardboiled eggs, chopped
8 tablespoons oil
2 tablespoons vinegar
salt and pepper to taste
2 tablespoons chopped parsley

(Serves 4–6)

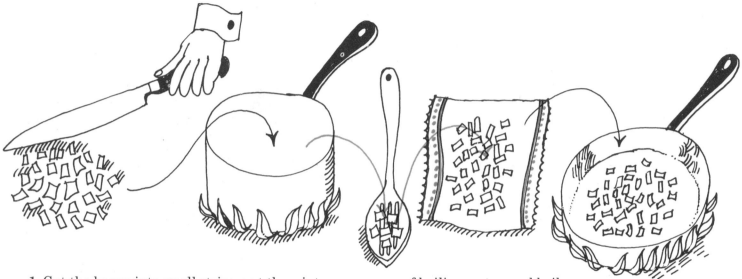

1 Cut the bacon into small strips, put them into a saucepan of boiling water, and boil them for 10 minutes to reduce the saltiness. Remove them with a slotted spoon and dry them on a paper towel. When thoroughly dry, fry the strips in the oil in a frying pan until crisp.

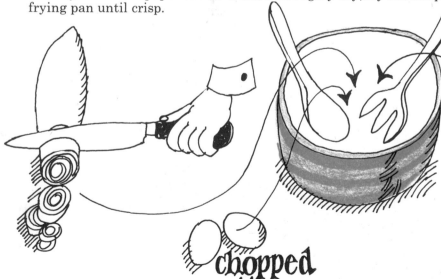

chopped egg

2 Cut the endive into ½-inch, thick slices and place them in a salad bowl. Add the chopped egg.

3 Make up the dressing of oil, vinegar, salt and pepper. Pour this mixture over the salad and toss it together gently but thoroughly.

4 Place it on a nice platter and sprinkle the bacon bits and parsley on top.

Serve very soon.

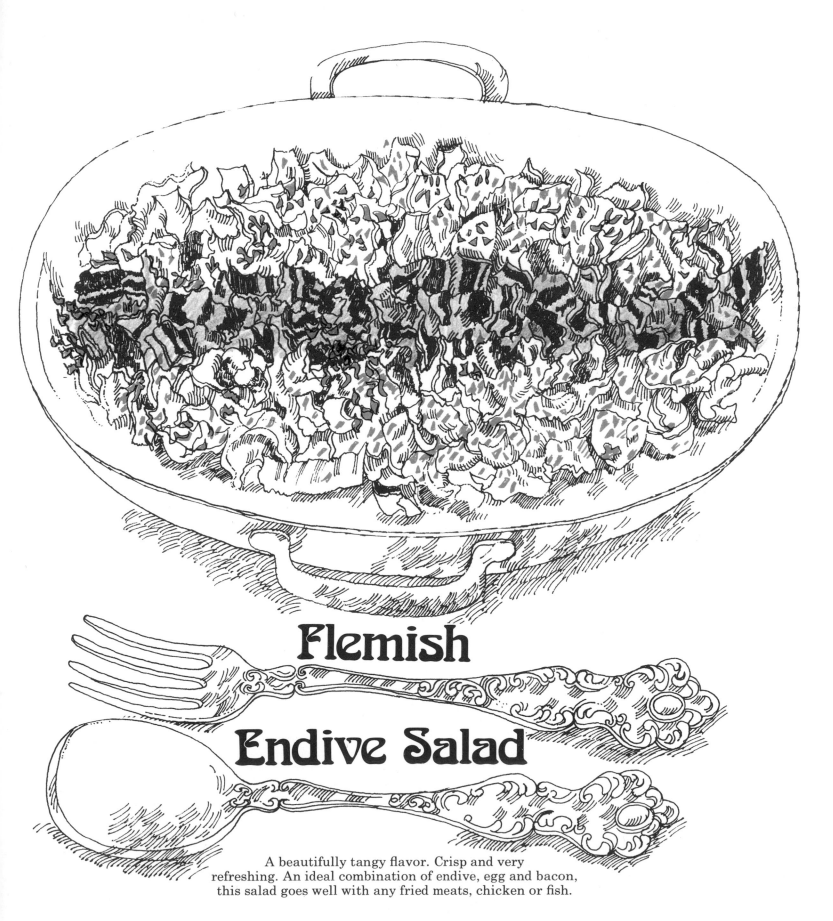

Flemish
Endive Salad

A beautifully tangy flavor. Crisp and very refreshing. An ideal combination of endive, egg and bacon, this salad goes well with any fried meats, chicken or fish.

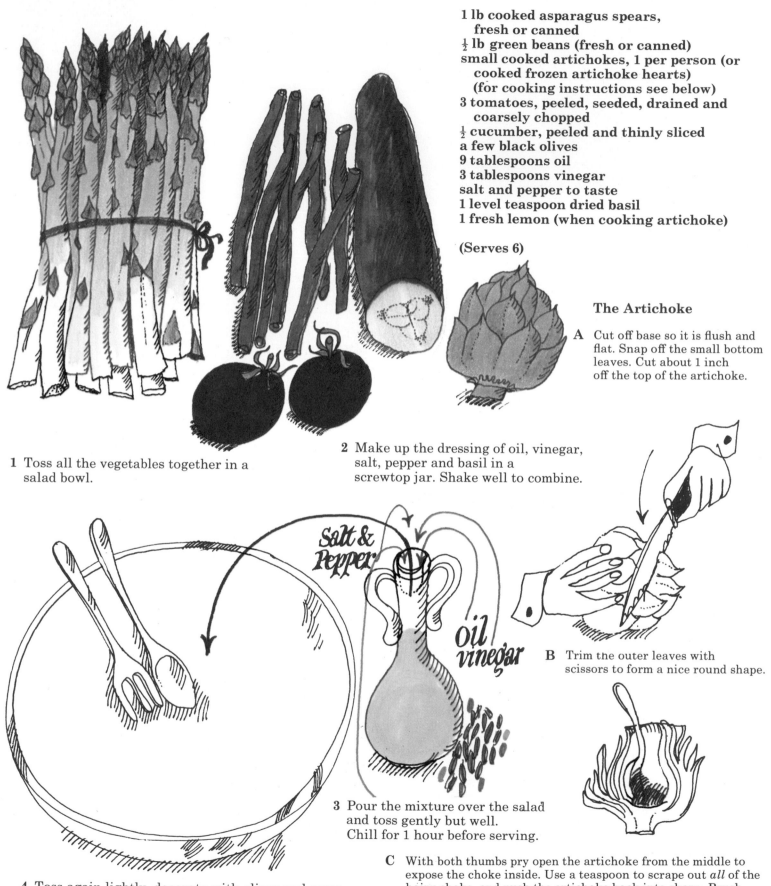

1 lb cooked asparagus spears,
   fresh or canned
½ lb green beans (fresh or canned)
small cooked artichokes, 1 per person (or
   cooked frozen artichoke hearts)
   (for cooking instructions see below)
3 tomatoes, peeled, seeded, drained and
   coarsely chopped
½ cucumber, peeled and thinly sliced
a few black olives
9 tablespoons oil
3 tablespoons vinegar
salt and pepper to taste
1 level teaspoon dried basil
1 fresh lemon (when cooking artichoke)

(Serves 6)

The Artichoke

A Cut off base so it is flush and flat. Snap off the small bottom leaves. Cut about 1 inch off the top of the artichoke.

1 Toss all the vegetables together in a salad bowl.

2 Make up the dressing of oil, vinegar, salt, pepper and basil in a screwtop jar. Shake well to combine.

Salt & Pepper

oil vinegar

B Trim the outer leaves with scissors to form a nice round shape.

3 Pour the mixture over the salad and toss gently but well. Chill for 1 hour before serving.

4 Toss again lightly, decorate with olives and serve from the salad bowl or transfer it to a platter.

C With both thumbs pry open the artichoke from the middle to expose the choke inside. Use a teaspoon to scrape out *all* of the hairy choke, and push the artichoke back into shape. Brush with lemon juice to prevent it discoloring and boil in salted water for 15 minutes. Drain and leave to cool before using.

Italian Summer Salad

A real Italian salad. A typically Mediterranean combination. This is truly a magnificent recipe, grand enough to stand as an elegant starter. Or it can make an unusual side dish to the main course.

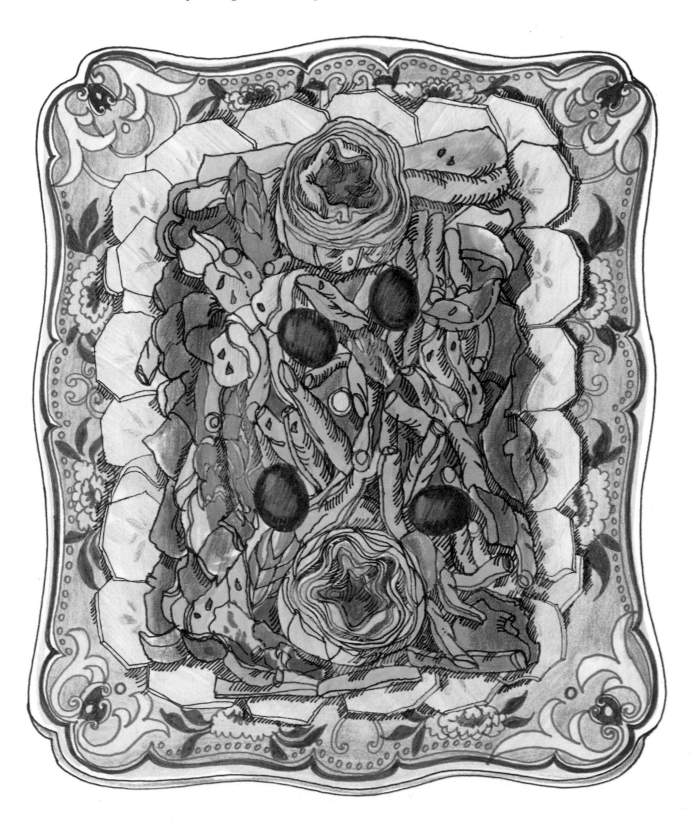

1 can salmon
2 heaped tablespoons very finely chopped
  celery
2 hardboiled eggs, chopped
4 tablespoons good mayonnaise
½ teaspoon curry powder

2 avocados
juice of 1 lemon
some nice lettuce leaves
paprika for garnish

(Serves 4)

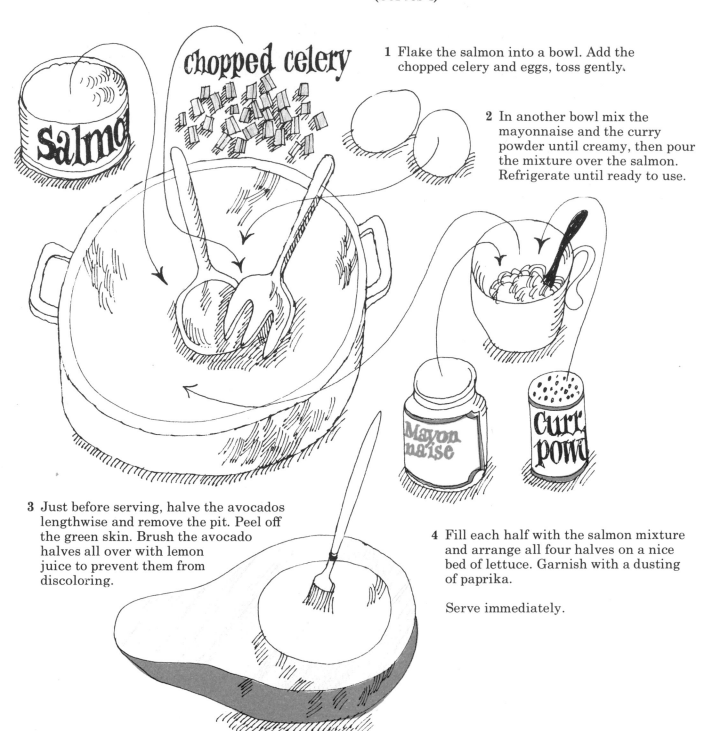

chopped celery

salmon

Mayonnaise

Curr powd

1 Flake the salmon into a bowl. Add the chopped celery and eggs, toss gently.

2 In another bowl mix the mayonnaise and the curry powder until creamy, then pour the mixture over the salmon. Refrigerate until ready to use.

3 Just before serving, halve the avocados lengthwise and remove the pit. Peel off the green skin. Brush the avocado halves all over with lemon juice to prevent them from discoloring.

4 Fill each half with the salmon mixture and arrange all four halves on a nice bed of lettuce. Garnish with a dusting of paprika.

Serve immediately.

Salmon & Avocado Salad

This makes an excellent hors d'oeuvre, winter and summer alike.
The smooth taste of the avocado blends ideally with the texture of
the salmon, eggs and celery. Very attractive to the eye.

1 small cucumber
¼ cup plus 2 tablespoons oil
5 tablespoons white wine vinegar
1 clove garlic, crushed
1 teaspoon dried basil
salt and pepper to taste
½ lb button mushrooms
5 spring onions, chopped
2 tablespoons chopped parsley
3 tomatoes, cut into wedges
1 green pepper, quartered, seeded and
   cut into strips

(Serves 4)

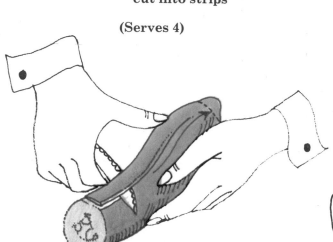

1 Peel the cucumber and cut it into thin slices.

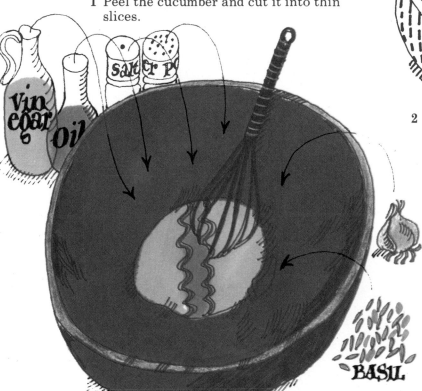

2 Place them in a colander, sprinkle some salt on top and leave to drain for 30 minutes. Rinse them with cold water and dry thoroughly.

3 In a large bowl make the dressing by combining the oil, vinegar, garlic, basil, salt and pepper thoroughly.

4 Add the whole mushrooms and chopped spring onions, the drained cucumber slices and the parsley, and toss all together gently. Chill in the refrigerator for an hour or more.

5 Place the tomato wedges over the salad in the bowl and over them the green pepper strips. Toss all the vegetables gently but thoroughly.

Serve immediately.

MEXICAN GAZPACHO SALAD

A super salad when served really fresh and slightly chilled. Juicy and refreshing. An ideal side dish to accompany any meat course.

1 head lettuce (any kind)
6 red radishes, cut into slices
2 tomatoes, cut into slices
2 celery stalks, chopped
½ cucumber, peeled and diced
6 stuffed green olives, sliced
1 bunch watercress, trimmed
½ lb cooked shrimp
   (fresh or frozen)
8 tablespoons oil

4 tablespoons vinegar
salt and pepper to taste
1 teaspoon dried tarragon
1 green pepper, cut into rings and seeded

(Serves 4–6)

1 Wash and dry the lettuce leaves and tear them into bite-size pieces. Place them in a salad bowl.

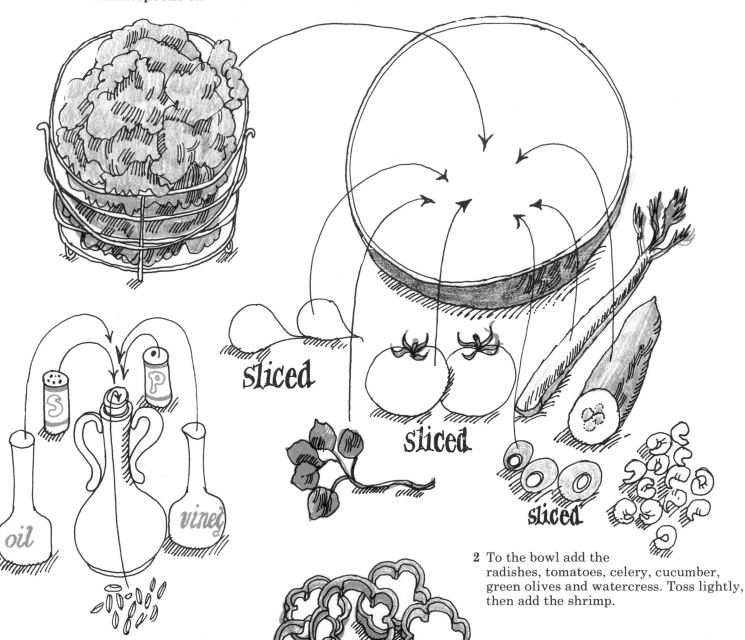

sliced

sliced

sliced

2 To the bowl add the radishes, tomatoes, celery, cucumber, green olives and watercress. Toss lightly, then add the shrimp.

3 Combine oil, vinegar, salt, pepper and tarragon in a screwtop jar, and shake well to combine. Pour it over the salad and toss well.

4 Garnish the tossed salad with the green pepper rings.

Serve immediately.

shrimp salad

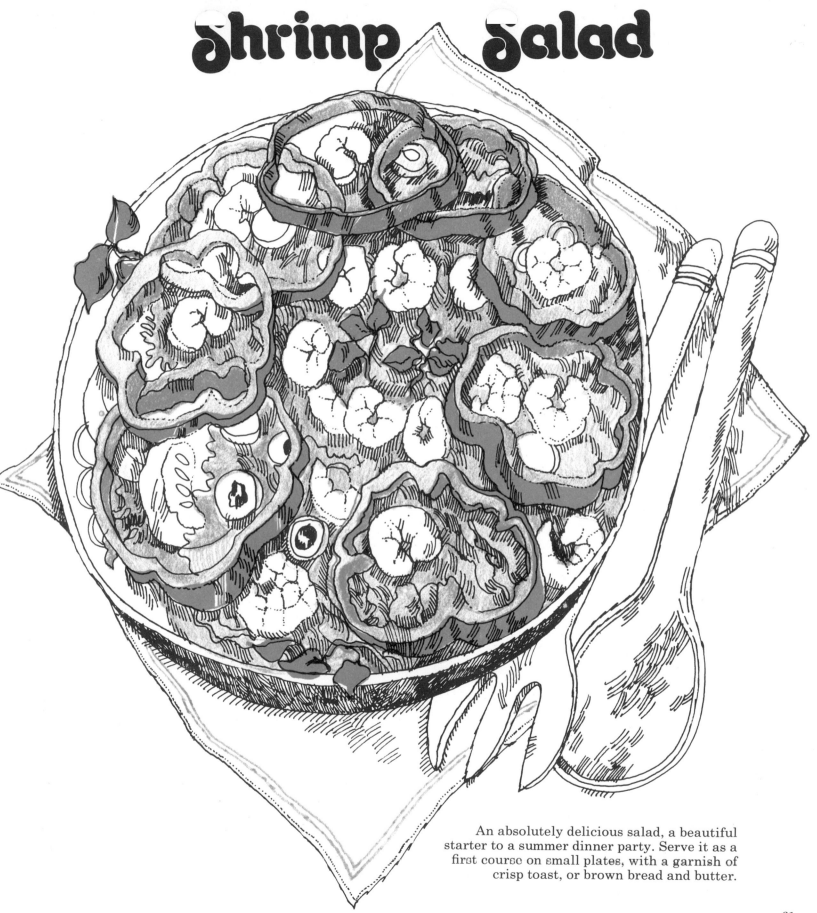

An absolutely delicious salad, a beautiful
starter to a summer dinner party. Serve it as a
first course on small plates, with a garnish of
crisp toast, or brown bread and butter.

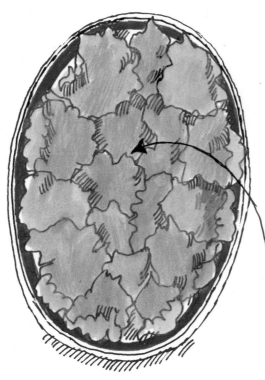

1 head lettuce
1 can crabmeat *or* ½ lb frozen crabmeat, cooked
6 heaped tablespoons good mayonnaise
4 tablespoons heavy cream
2 level teaspoons paprika
1 teaspoon Worcestershire sauce
5 spring onions, chopped
2 tablespoons fresh lemon juice
salt and pepper to taste
2 hardboiled eggs, cut into wedges
lemon wedges
1 tablespoon chopped parsley

(Serves 2 for lunch and 4 as an hors d'oeuvre)

crabmeat

2 Place the crabmeat in the centre of the platter and pour over it the following famous Louis dressing:

1 Arrange some perfect large lettuce leaves on a nice platter. Scatter the smaller leaves over them, or tear them into bite-size pieces.

3 In a small bowl gently mix the mayonnaise, cream, paprika, Worcestershire sauce, spring onions, lemon juice, salt and pepper until well blended.

4 Garnish with wedges of hardboiled egg and lemon and sprinkle with parsley.

Serve immediately.

CRAB SALAD LOUIS

A San Francisco classic, this salad has endeared itself to millions of Americans. The special dressing together with the crab meat gives this salad a typically San Francisco flavor. It can be served as a first course or as a delightful summer lunch. Fresh and satisfying, the flavor more than justifies the additional cost of preparing this salad.

SALAD DRESSINGS

Mayonnaise

1 egg yolk
¼ teaspoon dry mustard
salt and pepper to taste
pinch of sugar
2 tablespoons wine vinegar
¼ cup plus 2 tablespoons oil

Place the egg yolk, mustard, salt, pepper and sugar in a deep bowl. Mix until well combined. Add the vinegar and whisk it (with a wooden spoon or wire whisk) until white and frothy. Add the oil slowly, drop by drop, whisking constantly, until all the oil is used.
Occasionally the mayonnaise will curdle. Start again in another bowl with just one egg yolk. Whisk it constantly and slowly and add the curdled mayonnaise to it, by the teaspoonful, until it is all smooth and creamy. If the mayonnaise seems too thick for your needs, thin it down with a little cream. Mayonnaise can also be made in a blender. (Follow the directions in your blender book.) Mayonnaise made in a blender does not have the same shine and texture.

Green Goddess Dressing

1 recipe mayonnaise as above
3 chopped anchovy fillets
3 spring onions, chopped
2 tablespoons chopped parsley
1 teaspoon dried tarragon
1 heaped tablespoon chopped chives
2 tablespoons wine vinegar

Mix all the ingredients until smooth and creamy. Refrigerate before using on any green salad.

Thousand Island Dressing

1 recipe mayonnaise as above
5 tablespoons ketchup
8 stuffed olives, finely chopped
1 small green pepper, finely chopped
1 tablespoon finely chopped chives or onion
1 hardboiled egg, chopped
1 tablespoon chopped parsley

Mix all the ingredients together until smooth and creamy. Refrigerate before using on any green salad.

Yogurt Dressing

1 carton yogurt (8 oz)
1 small clove garlic, crushed
½ teaspoon dried oregano
1 tablespoon oil
salt and pepper to taste
1 fresh lemon (juice only)

Mix well, until smooth, the yogurt, crushed garlic, oregano, oil, salt and pepper. Then stir in the lemon juice and blend until smooth and creamy. (About 280 calories.)

Creamy French Dressing

1 tablespoon paprika
1 teaspoon sugar
1 teaspoon salt
6 tablespoons vinegar
1 raw egg
½ cup plus 2 tablespoons oil

Combine paprika, sugar and salt. Add the vinegar and the egg and beat well. Add the oil in a slow stream, beating all the time, until the mixture is thick and creamy. Chill before serving over any green salad.

Blue Cheese Dressing

1 clove garlic
4 oz blue cheese
2 teaspoons Worcestershire sauce
juice of 1 lemon
½ teaspoon dry mustard
¼ teaspoon paprika
1 tablespoon oil
salt and pepper to taste
1 recipe mayonnaise as above

Mash garlic and cheese in a bowl. Add the Worcestershire sauce, lemon juice, mustard, paprika, oil, salt and pepper. Blend well. Add the mayonnaise and stir until smooth and creamy. Refrigerate before using over any green salad.

Watercress Dressing

2 tablespoons fresh lemon juice
1 tablespoon wine vinegar
½ teaspoon dried tarragon
¼ cup plus 2 tablespoons oil
salt and pepper to taste
1 bunch watercress

Mix lemon juice, vinegar, tarragon, oil, salt and pepper until well blended. Then stir in 1 bunch of finely chopped watercress. Use over any green salad.

Low Calorie Dressing

8 oz cottage cheese
¼ cup plus 2 tablespoons milk
salt and pepper to taste
2 tablespoons fresh lemon juice
1 small green pepper, chopped
5 spring onions, chopped
1 clove garlic, crushed

You can best do this in a blender. Just swirl all the ingredients around until well blended. Refrigerate before using on any green salad.
If a blender is not available, force the cottage cheese through a fine sieve, and add all the other ingredients to it. Blend until smooth. (About 350 calories.)